THE BIBLE

THE MIRACULOUS WORD OF GOD

by

DR. STEVE KERN

For more information contact
Kern Enterprises
2713 N. Sterling Ave.
Oklahoma City, OK 73127
(405) 308-0412

All scripture references are from
the New American Standard Bible,
translated by Lockman Foundation.

(Parentheses within quoted Bible verses
are added by the author.)

ISBN: 978-0-9798667-8-4

Contents

Foreword 7

Introduction 9

Chapter 1 Light and Dark 13

Chapter 2 Coverings 22

Chapter 3 Weddings 37

Chapter 4 Miracles 46

Chapter 5 Prophecies 59

Chapter 6 Messiah 67

Chapter 7 Redemption 75

Conclusion 81

Foreword

I first met Steve Kern when our church had the privilege of helping with his ministry to women trying to establish themselves and their children after serving time in prison. Steve is a doer of the Word and not a hearer only. He loves the Bible, and he does the Bible.

When we love someone or something, we want others to share that love. Steve writes so that we will share his love and wonder for God's Word. His love for the Bible radiates from every page of this book. Steve believes the Bible, and he wants you to share this conviction. I think this work will help you. He makes a strong case for the beauty, the wonder, and the miracle of the Bible, God's Word.

I knew Steve Kern as pastor and preacher, but I did not know he is also a poet. His poetry brought to mind a little book written by W. A. Criswell in 1965, "The Bible for Today's World." That book includes a poem by John Clifford.

Last eve I paused beside the blacksmith's door
And heard the anvil ring the vesper chime;
Then looking in, I saw upon the floor,
Old hammers, worn with beating years of time.
"How many anvils have you had," said I,
"To wear and batter all these hammers so?"
"Just one," said he, and then with twinkling eye,
"The anvil wears the hammers out, you know."
And so, I thought, the Anvil of God's Word,
For ages skeptic blows have beat upon;
Yet, though the noise of falling blows was heard,
The Anvil is unharmed, the hammers gone.

Hance Dilbeck
Executive Director-Treasurer
Oklahoma Baptists
May 14, 2020

Introduction

The Bible is miraculous because its existence can only be explained by divine inspiration that exceeds the ability of limited human creativity. Miracle is the only plausible explanation for this library of 66 books, written over a period of 4,000 years, by 40 different men, in separated periods of time, in the midst of different circumstances, even different countries. Yet, it is totally consistent with itself in historical development, archeological discovery, and themes within that continue from beginning to end. It demands a single source of intelligent inspiration that is not limited to space or time. Of course that source must be the God we are introduced to by the Bible itself in its very first sentence, "In the beginning God (Elohim) created the heavens and the earth." These words were probably written by God Himself or passed on by direct verbal inspiration. If you want to know why I believe this to be true, read my book "No Other Gods." The major point of this book is: Given the Bible's diverse background of development over thousands of years; and that it is totally consistent with itself from beginning to end in message and themes, it surely is the miraculous Word of God.

It is not my objective to discuss the historical development of the Bible or archeological discoveries that affirm the Bible's authenticity. There are many books, including "No Other Gods" and "The Genesis Record" by Dr. Henry Morris, that have been written based on these topics that give ample instruction on understanding them. Instead I want to cover some of the major themes in the Bible that are introduced from the Bible's beginnings and can be traced through its different books all the way through Revelation. The interesting observation that can be made about each of these themes is that they are established in the beginning of God's Word as pictorial prophecies that point to God's ultimate fulfilled purposes at the end. What you find introduced in the beginning you find complete in the end.

It is my hope that as you follow these themes you will deepen your conviction that the Bible is the Word of God and can be trusted to be His divine revelation. And, that it can be trusted to bring about His ultimate plan of redemption of mankind. Thus, in doing so, His kingdom will be established for eternity, totally good with the total absence of evil. It is my prayer that this book will help you to know the Bible is God's Word and in having that knowledge you will believe it and live your life according to its instruction.

I will cover the following 7 major themes:

- Light and Dark
- Coverings
- Weddings
- Miracles
- Prophecies
- Messiah
- Redemption

There are other themes, but I plan to use these 7 to show how God's Word is totally consistent with itself and is a continual ongoing revelation of God and His plan of redemption from beginning to end connected by these themes. I will show how God's redemptive plan was established from the beginning and will be totally completed in the end. My message is, JUST BELIEVE GOD'S WORD! Why? Because it is a miraculous inspired message given by God Himself, with the intent of being a blessing to those willing to believe it comes from him.

I want to thank my wife, Sally, for suggesting that I write this book.

Chapter 1
Light and Dark

*"And this is the judgment,
that the light is come into the world,
and men loved the darkness
rather than the light..."*
John 3:19

The first theme we will look at is Light and Dark. The first recorded spoken words by God in His Word are, "Let there be light..." Genesis 1:3. They were spoken on the first day of God's creative work. Then we are told the light was good after it was separated from the darkness in verse 4. God's Word is what scholars describe as a progressive revelation. As God's Word progresses He gives us more and more information about Himself and His creative purposes. When it comes to light, we learn that light emanates from God. It is not created but is produced by God's very being. Light comes from the very essence of who God is.

It seems that when God separated the light from the darkness on the first day of creation that this action was prophetic. All was created by God very good; but after the fall of man into sin by the deception of Satan, light became the symbol of what is good, righteous, and true before God; and in contrast dark became the symbol of what is evil, detestable, and deceptive from Satan. From then on God's Word becomes a commentary on the struggle between light and darkness that distinguishes between the ways of God and the ways of Satan. It is an ongoing war between good and evil that is moving to an ultimate climax. This was predicted in Genesis 1:4 when God separated the light from the dark.

In the Old Testament during the Exodus, God gives two symbols of His presence using light. There was the pillar of fire by night and cloud of smoke by day that was the presence of God leading the way for the Israelites through the wilderness. The pillar of fire gave God's light in the darkness. The other symbol was the lampstand with its seven branches that stood in the tabernacle and then the temple in the Holy Place across from the table of showbread. There were no windows to let light into the Holy Place. The lampstand gave the only light symbolizing the presence of God. The lampstand has become the symbol of the nation of Israel as God's chosen people.

These two symbols are referred to in different parts of the Old Testament as reminders of God's faithfulness amongst His people in their history. Nehemiah 9:12 says, "And with a pillar of cloud Thou didst lead them by day, and with a pillar of fire by night to light for them the way in which they were to go." King David refers to the lampstand in his Psalm of Praise recorded in 2 Samuel 22:29, "For Thou art my lamp, O Lord, and the Lord illumines my darkness."

In the Psalms, light is used to refer to God and His truth often such as in Psalm 27:1, "The Lord is my light and my salvation; whom shall I fear?" Psalm 18:28 also says, "...for Thou doest light my lamp; the Lord my God illumines my darkness." The prophets also use light to refer to God. Isaiah 60:20, "Your sun will set no more, neither will your moon wane; for you will have the Lord for an everlasting light, and the days of your mourning will be finished." Micah 7:8 also states boldly, "Do not rejoice over me, O my enemy. Though I fall I will rise; though I dwell in darkness, the Lord is a light for me." We will see that these and many other prophecies like them will be fulfilled in Revelation 21 and 22.

One of the most important prophecies that uses light to refer to the coming of the Messiah, Jesus, and infers that this great light will be God Himself coming to live amongst His creation as the light, is Isaiah 9:2, "The people who walk in darkness will see a great light; those who live in a dark land, the light will shine on them." This theme of the Messiah being the light of God is taken up in the New Testament. Jesus uses it to refer to Himself often in His teachings as well.

The major verse in the New Testament that defines God as light, which helps us understand the light in Genesis 1:3, "Let there be light," as being the light of God Himself is 1 John 1:5. John states clearly, "And this is the message that we have heard from Him and announce to you, that God is light, and in Him is no darkness at all." It is this same John the apostle who in his gospel introduction refers back to the creation week by describing Jesus as a part of the Godhead as the Word who is the "life and light of mankind." James 1:17 also refers to God as the "Father of lights," meaning the light from the sun, moon, and stars was made possible by God's very own light. In other words the light in Genesis 1:3 was the light of God's very own presence that emanates from His being. We know this because the light holders as they are called were not created until three days later. Before the fourth day, God's light was all there was.

In John 8:12 Jesus claims to be the God of Genesis 1:3 when He declared, "I am the light of the world..." The "I Am" refers to God when He told Moses what to tell the people of Israel: His name is, "I Am" the eternal present. The light of the world refers to the light that was given by God when He said, "Let there be light" in Genesis 1:3. Jesus goes on to say in the rest of that verse, "...he who follows Me will not walk in the darkness, but shall have the light of life." Jesus here claims to be the truth or light of God revealed in the books of the Old Testament. When we obey God's Word by putting our faith in Jesus He gives us the way to living the kind of life that rejects all the lies of Satan's darkness.

The rest of the New Testament books beyond the Gospels often refer to the theme of light and dark. In Acts 26:18 Paul gives his testimony of being called by Jesus to take the Gospel to the Gentiles, "I am sending you, to open their eyes so that they may turn from darkness to light and from the dominion of Satan to God, in order that they may receive forgiveness of sins and an inheritance among those who have been sanctified by faith in Me." Paul uses the light theme in 2 Corinthians 6:14 as well, " Do not be bound together with unbelievers; for what partnership has righteousness (Jesus) and lawlessness (Satan), or what fellowship has light with darkness?" Peter in 1 Peter 2:9 uses the light theme to describe the Church where he wrote, "But you are a chosen race, a royal priesthood, a holy nation, a people for God's own possession, that you may proclaim the excellencies of Him who has called you out of darkness into His marvelous light..."

The culmination of the light and dark theme being an example of how God's Word is consistent with itself is found in Revelation. I stated at the beginning of this chapter that Genesis 1:4 is a prophecy statement of what God will finally accomplish at the end of His plan for His creation. Remember, Genesis 1:4 took place 4,000 years before Revelation was written. At the end of Revelation we see that finally God separates the light from the darkness once for all. God's Word ends where it begins with light being separated from darkness. A war begins between good and evil at the fall of man and God finally wins in the end with the establishment of the new heaven and earth.

As the book of Revelation comes to the end of the tribulation and the millennial reign of Jesus, Satan is released from the pit after a thousand years for one final attempt to defeat Jesus and the people of God who love the light. Satan is finally thrown into the lake of fire along with all those who followed his dark ways, as Revelation 20:10-15 reveals.

Hell in the Bible is described as a terrible place of torment and total darkness. In Matthew 8:12 Jesus gives this description of Hell, "...but the sons of the kingdom (unbelieving Jews) shall be cast out into the outer darkness, in that place there shall be weeping and gnashing of teeth." Obviously the place He is referring to is Hell. So in the end all those who loved the darkness in this life will spend eternity in darkness along with Satan and all his demonic spirits.

Then we come to Revelation 21 and 22. There we see a place of total light and no dark at all, where God Himself is the source of the light. Revelation 21:23 gives this description of the New Jerusalem in the new heaven and earth, "And the city has no need of the sun or of the moon to shine upon it, for the glory of God has illumined it, and its lamp is the Lamb." Revelation 22:5 gives more information, "And there shall no longer be any night; and they shall not have need of the light of a lamp nor the light of the sun, because the Lord God shall illumine them; and they shall reign forever and ever." These verses tell us that those who love the light will live in the eternal light of the Lord God.

When considering the consistency of God's Word with itself, we see, as I said earlier, that God's Word ends where it begins. God spoke "Let there be light," which was a declaration of God committing Himself to light His creation. Remember this was on the first day. The sun, moon and stars were not created until the fourth day. So it was God Himself illuminating the earth for the first three days. Again, we see then in Revelation 21 and 22 that the new heaven and earth will be illuminated by God Himself once again just as it was in the first three days of the creation week, only this time it will be for eternity. Darkness will have been removed once and for all. The prophecy of Genesis 1:4, "and God separated the light from the dark..." is finally fulfilled once and for all. The theme of light and dark from the beginning to the end of God's Word shows God illuminated the whole process. God's Word is consistent with itself because God is consistent with Himself. God's word is miraculous.

I wrote the following poem about what the theme of Light and Dark teaches us:

LIGHT OR DARK

We each must take our turn
As the earth in time does turn
To show what is in our heart
Love for the light or for dark
This was shown from the start
Light separated from dark
The light was declared good
Opposed to the dark it stood
What does love for light show?
A love for God, Him to know
What does love for dark show?
A love for self as God's foe
What is each destiny?
To spend for eternity
Lovers of light in heaven dwell
Lovers of dark in darkest Hell
So what is in your heart?
Love for light or love for dark?
Jesus' light draws those near
Whose love for light is sincere

Genesis 1:4 / John 3:19-21
Steve Kern 6/4/2018

Chapter 2
Coverings

*"Blessed are those whose lawless
deeds have been forgiven,
and whose sins have been covered."*
Romans 4:7

The next theme I want to discuss is what I call Coverings. I originally planned to call it Atonement because the word in the Hebrew for atonement can be translated covering. I decided to use the word "covering" because I believe we relate to the concept of covering more readily than atonement. There are five distinct coverings expressed in the Bible that make up this theme that is another example of how God's Word is consistent with itself from beginning to end. It gives support to the concept of God's sovereign direction of the writing of the books of the Bible from the first to the last. God is the single guiding force behind the Bible's development.

The five coverings are:
- The Water Canopy
- The Animal Skins
- Noah's Ark
- The Day of Atonement
- Jesus Christ

The covering theme is also a principle in God's Word. The principle can be stated as follows: "God provides protection for those who are under His grace and mercy." In other words, God protects those who love and obey Him and live in dependence on Him for all their needs. For those who are vulnerable and depending on God, God provides His protective covering. That protection can be removed when God determines it necessary according to His purposes or due to disobedience and sin.

The Water Canopy

The water canopy is the first covering given on the second day of creation in Genesis 1:6-7, "Then God said, 'Let there be an expanse in the midst of the waters, and let it separate the waters from the waters.' And God made the expanse, and separated the waters which were below the expanse from the waters which were above the expanse; and it was so." These verses tell us that after the first day the earth was a sphere of water rotating, because there was an "evening and morning the first day." The second day involved the formation of the atmosphere rising out of the water that lifts a portion of water above the atmosphere providing a protective covering. This covering encased the atmosphere and sphere of water that will become the land, seas, vegetation, animals, and man on the earth.

We do not know what form the water above the atmosphere took. Was it a liquid, ice, vapor, or a plasma? The most reasonable guess would be water vapor. A vapor canopy, as it is called, would be clear to see through, lighter than the atmosphere in order to be held above it, and would add weight above the atmosphere. This added weight would create a heavier atmospheric pressure that would increase positive environmental qualities, and the canopy would also deflect negative light rays coming from the sun that cause mutations in DNA. In other words the water canopy covering would make life on earth absent of negative health issues. There would be no clouds, no rain, moderate temperatures thus no storms, and no polar icecaps. You can read a full explanation of this water canopy in Dr. Henry Morris's book, "The Genesis Record" pages 57-61. You can also read about it in my book, "No Other Gods" in chapter 4.

The water canopy provided a life-enriching and sustaining environment for all of God's creation for 1556 years until it was condensed into rain during the worldwide flood catastrophe. We are told in Genesis 7:11 that "the fountains of the great deep were broken up." The water trapped underground in large aquifers was under great pressure that broke up the earth's crust. It then exploded into the upper atmosphere causing the water canopy to condense into rain. There was so much water in the canopy that the rain fell for 40 days and nights. The environmental change that took place after its removal was catastrophic. The four seasons were ushered in. The length of life began to shorten. The polar icecaps began to form. An ice age took place for several hundred years. Deserts began to form as the water dried up. Cataclysmic storms began to rage and they continue to rage to this day. Earthquakes began to rumble all over the earth as the broken up earth crust began to settle. The crust continues to settle to this day.

Thankfully, there are hints in the Old Testament that the water canopy will be restored at the beginning of the millennial reign of Christ after the tribulation. It was removed because the sin of mankind had become so out of control that the flood was necessary for God to bring it back under control. He then started over so He could continue His plan of redemption that we will discuss later.

In the end we see a new heaven and earth where God dwells with mankind in a totally perfect environment similar to the one made possible by the water canopy covering in the first heaven and earth. Only the new heaven and earth will be protected and sustained by the very presence of God Himself in person with the Tree of Life and a river of crystal clear water that flows from God's throne. All of these are reminders of how things were in the Garden of Eden before the fall. All this anticipates God's fulfilled final purpose in the new heaven and earth. All will have been made new.

Animal Skins

Animal skins is the second covering and is found in Genesis 3:21, "And the Lord God made garments of skin for Adam and his wife, and clothed them." This verse comes after the curses on the serpent, Eve, Adam, and the ground that would produce "thorns and thistles." There was also the curse of death, which the animals slain by God for their shed blood and their skins were the first to suffer. After Adam and Eve had eaten of the forbidden fruit, they realized they were naked and tried to cover themselves with fig leaves. The shame of nakedness became the reminder of their fallen position in relationship with Holy God.

God in His grace prepared garments to accomplish three things. First, He covered their shame in His presence to emphasize His holiness to Adam and Eve. Second, knowing He would have to force them to leave the garden, taking away their access to the Tree of Life, He gave Adam and Eve the protective covering of animal skins to protect them from the thorns and thistles. They would now have to endure the hostile environment they were going to be living in from then on. Third, this act of slaying the animals, and shedding their blood was a lesson teaching, what the Law of Moses would reemphasize many years later, that the shedding of blood is the only way to receive forgiveness of sins. From then on animals would have to be sacrificed to cover man's sins until the ultimate sacrifice would come in the person of Jesus Christ, God's Son.

Clothing has been the standard ever since that time, used for protective covering against the elements of a hostile earth and to express a person's modesty. An evolutionistic worldview based on the idea that humans are just more advanced animals cannot explain where this reality of shame and need to express modesty comes from. They are qualities not found in the animal kingdom, but are very real to fallen human beings created in the image of Holy God.

Clothing is found throughout the Bible. God Himself is described as wearing clothing in different passages. Psalm 93:1 says, "The Lord reigns, He is clothed with majesty; the Lord has clothed and girded Himself with strength…" Psalm 104:1-2 gives a similar description, "…O Lord my God, Thou art very great; Thou art clothed with splendor and majesty, covering Thyself with light as with a cloak…" Ezekiel 1:26 gives a further description of God clothed with light, "… and on that which resembled a throne, high up, was a figure with the appearance of a man. Then I noticed from the appearance of His loins and upward something like glowing metal that looked like fire all around within it, and from the appearance of His loins and downward I saw something like fire; and there was a radiance around Him."

In Exodus 28 God gives instructions to Moses about how the priests are to clothe themselves while serving in the tabernacle. In the instructions there is an emphasis on maintaining modesty and covering the nakedness that symbolized the fallen state of all mankind that came about by Adam and Eve's disobedience to God's command. The verse is Exodus 28: 42-43, "And you shall make for them linen breeches to cover their bare flesh; they shall reach from the loins even to the thighs. And they shall be on Aaron and on his sons when they enter the tent of meeting, or when they approach the alter to minister in the holy place, so that they do not incur guilt and die..." The robes of the priests were to be long enough to cover their ankles and they were not to walk up steps so their ankles were not exposed as a part of their nakedness. Exodus 20:26, "And you shall not go up by steps to My alter, that your nakedness not be exposed on it."

When we come to Revelation 1:13 we are given a picture of the resurrected Jesus dressed similar to the High Priest in Exodus 28, "...and in the middle of the lampstands one like a Son of Man, clothed in a robe reaching to His feet, and girded across His breast with a golden girdle." In Revelation 7:13-14 we see a vast congregation dressed in white robes and we are told why they can wear them, "...These who are clothed in the white robes, who are they and from where have they come? And I said to him, My lord, you know. And he said to me, these are the ones who come out of the great tribulation, and they have washed their robes and made them white in the blood of the Lamb (Jesus)."

When we come to the end of Revelation we find that believers have been clothed by God in white robes of righteousness rather than the bloody skins of animals. The white robes were made possible by God the Father allowing His only Son to shed His blood to cover man's sin once and for all. So, now we can be clothed in the white robes of the righteousness of Jesus. Revelation 19:8 says, "And it was given to her (the Church) to clothe herself in fine linen, bright and clean..." Revelation 19:14 goes on to say, "And the armies which are in heaven (believers in Jesus) clothed in fine linen white and clean, were following Him (Jesus) on white horses." What was prophetic in Genesis 3:21 is completed in Revelation. This was all made possible by the guidance of the Holy Spirit inspiring men to write what was to become God's Word being consistent with itself from beginning to end. Adam and Eve were clothed by God through the broken body and shed blood of sacrificed animals. Christians will be clothed by God in Heaven through the broken body and shed blood of God's Son, Jesus Christ.

Noah's Ark

The third covering is Noah's ark. The ark is given by God to be a covering of protection from God's coming judgment against a world that became totally depraved beyond God's grace and mercy. God gave instructions to Noah, the only righteous man left on earth, on how to build the ark that would take 120 years to build. During that time Noah preached con- cerning God's coming judgment but only his family listened and were willing to enter the ark.

There is an interesting word in Genesis 6:14. The word is translated "pitch" in English but is the word for "atonement" in the Hebrew. The verse says, "Make for yourself an ark of gopher wood; you shall make the ark with rooms, and shall cover it inside and out with pitch." Dr Henry Morris explains the translation as follows, "The word for 'pitch' (Hebrew kopher) is different from that used in other places in the Old Testament. It is equivalent to the Hebrew kaphar (to cover) and, in the noun form, means simply a 'covering.' However, it is also the regular Hebrew word for 'atonement' as in Leviticus 17:11, for example. In essence, therefore, this is the first mention of 'atonement' in the Bible." (The Genesis Record pp. 181-182)

The flood and Noah's ark is referred to often in the Old and New Testament. The ark was to be the protective covering God would provide for those who were under His grace and mercy in the midst of His judgment. It was available for anyone to come and enter; but only eight souls finally did enter. 2 Peter 2:5 says, "...(God) did not spare the ancient world, but preserved Noah, a preacher of righteousness, with seven others, when He brought a flood upon the world of the ungodly..." Psalm 29:10, "The Lord sat as King at the flood; Yes, the Lord sits as King forever." Jesus referred to the flood and judgment as a historical comparison to His second coming in Matthew 24:37-39, "For the coming of the Son of Man will be just like the days of Noah. For as in those days which were before the flood they were eating and drinking, they were marrying and giving in marriage, until the day that Noah entered the ark, and they did not understand until the flood came and took them all away, so shall the coming of the Son of Man be."

Once again the ark becomes a prophetic picture of how God has brought about His ultimate plan of redemption. Peter makes a comparison of how Jesus has become the ark of protection for Christians from God's coming fiery judgment. The apostle Peter, in 1 Peter 3:21, referred to Noah and his family being saved from judgment as mentioned in the previous verse 20, and compares that to how a Christian is baptized into Christ Jesus at salvation. "And corresponding to that (being in the ark), baptism (into Christ) now saves you – not the removal of dirt from the flesh (not water baptism) but an appeal to God for a good conscience – through the resurrection of Jesus Christ." Our good conscience comes from being forgiven of our sins and being immersed in Jesus. Being in Jesus, we are safe from God's coming judgment. Paul makes a similar point in Romans 6:3-4, "Or do you not know that all of us who have been baptized into Christ Jesus have been baptized into His death? Therefore we have been buried with Him through baptism into death, in order that as Christ was raised from the dead through the glory of the Father, so we might walk in newness of life."

Just as the ark carried Noah and his family safely through the flood, Jesus is the ark for all Christians whom He will carry safely through God's final judgment spoken of in Revelation 20:15, "... the lake of fire..." Christians are saved from that judgment because their names are written in "the Lamb's (Jesus's) book of life." They are safe in Jesus. The ark is another consistent covering in God's Word from beginning to end.

The Day of Atonement

The fourth covering is The Day of Atonement. We have seen in our other discussions of coverings that God established blood as the only covering for sin. When God chose Israel, the descendents of Abraham, to be His people amongst all the nations, He liberated them from slavery in Egypt. Then before He took them into the land of Canaan, He brought them to Mount Sinai to give them laws to follow as people serving a Holy God. Because God is holy and the people were fallen in sin, God established The Day of Atonement so as a Holy God He could maintain His presence amongst them.

This was a day once a year when the high priest made blood sacrifices for himself, the other priests of his household, and all the people to cover their sins. As has already been stated, atonement means covering. This day, the tenth day of the seventh month, was the only day of the year when the high priest alone was allowed to go behind the veil of the Holy of Holies to sprinkle the blood of a bull and a ram for himself and his household, and the blood of a goat for the people on the mercy seat sitting on the ark of the covenant. The high priest would then lay his hands on another goat called the scapegoat and confess all the sins of the people. This was a symbolic act of transferring all those sins to the scapegoat, sins that were atoned for by the other goat that was sacrificed. The scapegoat was then led into the wilderness and turned loose to carry the sins of the people away.

The Day of Atonement of course is a prophetic picture of the coming sacrifice of the Son of God who would come and take away the sins of the world. This same sacrifice is prophesied in Isaiah 53:6 that the Messiah will be the ultimate scapegoat, "All of us like sheep has gone astray, each of us has turned to his own way, but the Lord has caused the iniquity of us all to fall on Him." Hebrews 9:11-12 describes how Jesus fulfilled The Day of Atonement in the tabernacle of God in heaven, "But when Christ appeared as a high priest of the good things to come, He entered through the greater and more perfect tabernacle, not made with hands, that is to say, not of this creation; and not through the blood of goats and calves, but through His own blood, He entered the holy place once for all, having obtained eternal redemption." There are many other verses especially in the New Testament that allude to Jesus being the fulfillment of The Day of Atonement.

Jesus Christ

The fifth and final covering we will look at is Jesus Christ Himself. As we have already seen Jesus is the ultimate fulfillment of each of the above discussed coverings. This is to be expected because Jesus makes the point that all of scripture is about Him just as He told the disciples in the Upper Room after His resurrection in Luke 24:44, "Now He said to them, 'These are the words which I spoke to you while I was still with you, that all things which are written about Me in the Law of Moses and the Prophets and the Psalms must be fulfilled.'" When Jesus comes again after the tribulation to reign for a thousand years on earth, the water canopy will apparently be reestablished. People will once again live long periods of time. Carnivorous animals will eat straw again. A child will lead them. Deadly snakes will no longer be poisonous. Planting and harvesting will be year around. The environment will be as it was before the flood.

God slayed the animals to provide a protective covering with their skins for Adam and Eve after their fall and the curse of thorns and thistles. Jesus Christ through His broken body and shed blood provides a protective covering for our sins in a hostile world. Jesus is the ark that God places us in to protect us from the coming judgment of fire. Peter wrote in 1 Peter 3:18, "For Christ also died for sins once for all, the just for the unjust, in order that He might bring (carry) us to God." Just as the ark carried Noah and his family to safety, Jesus will bring those of us in Him to eternal safety. And finally, Jesus is the sacrificial atonement that fulfills the prophetic Day of Atonement just as He is the fulfillment of the sacrificial Passover Lamb on the day He shed His blood on the cross. Jesus is our covering who was prophetically portrayed pictorally in God's Word from beginning to end. God's word is miraculously beyond human comprehension.

Chapter 3
Weddings

"Go therefore to the main highways ,
and as many as you find there,
invite them to the wedding feast."
Matthew 22:9

There are four new beginnings in the Bible and each one begins with our next theme, Weddings.

This theme develops from the beginning of Genesis to the end of Revelation. The four weddings in our theme are:

- Adam and Eve
- God and Israel
- Cana
- Christ and the Church

Adam and Eve

The first wedding took place in the Garden of Eden. The couple to be joined together in holy matrimony was the newly created Adam and Eve. The one who officiated was the very Creator Himself. Eve was taken out of the side of Adam. When God brought Eve to Adam after He had awakened him from his God-imposed sleep, Adam's response was, "This is now bone of my bones, and flesh of my flesh; she shall be called Woman, because she was taken out of man." Then there is an added statement given possibly by God Himself, "for this cause a man shall leave his father and mother, and shall cleave to his wife; and they shall become one flesh." Genesis 2:23-24.

It is important to note that this wedding ceremony took place immediately after Adam and Eve's creation and at the very beginning of their living their lives out together. It is clear that Adam was not to find pleasure or satisfaction from the animals after naming some of them to learn he was not an animal. He had a deeper relationship need that could only be met by another human that was like him yet different. It is also clear that it was God's intent to establish a moral standard of relationship as one man and one woman living and procreating together for life. Any activity outside of this marital standard was not ordained by God and after the fall would be considered immoral and ungodly. It was God's intent for His creation to become full of human beings who were produced by a man and a woman committed to each other unto God to produce a family of godly seed. This was all to be done by Adam and Eve living as free moral agents choosing to live according to God's designed purpose for the inhabitation of His perfect God honoring creation.

God gave Adam and Eve the mandate in Genesis 1:28, "And God blessed them; and God said to them, 'Be fruitful and multiply, and fill the earth'..." They were to have children and when their children were grown their sons would marry a wife and they would start their family. That was to be God's holy standard for populating the earth; a husband and a wife were to be as one with each other made in God's image producing godly seed.

After the fall into sin by Adam and Eve, God's purpose for marriage deteriorated rapidly and sexual immorality became common practice. Polygamy, adultery, divorce, fornication, prostitution, homosexuality, bestiality; all these acts of illicit sex distorted God's purpose for human sexuality and the family. But the first wedding became a prophetic picture of God's future plan for His eternal kingdom.

God and Israel

The second wedding is God's marriage to Israel at Mount Sinai. The following are a few verses that suggest the husband/wife relationship between God and Israel. In Ezekiel 16:8 God reminisces about how He found Israel in need and married her,"...I also swore to you and entered into a covenant (marriage vows) with you so that you became mine." Isaiah 54:5 says, "...for your husband is your Maker, Whose name is the Lord of hosts..." Verse 6 goes on to say, "For the Lord has called you, like a wife forsaken and grieved in spirit, even like a wife of one's youth when she is rejected." Jeremiah 31:32 refers to the Mount Sinai covenant and God being Israel's husband, "...My covenant which they broke, although I was a husband to them, declares the Lord."

In Judaism, the meeting of Israel with God at Mount Sinai is seen as a wedding ceremony of both parties entering into a covenant agreement to live together as husband and wife. The Law was given by God along with His promises of blessings to protect and provide for Israel. Betrothed Israel agreed to the covenant in Exodus 19:8 with Moses acting as the friend of the bridegroom, "And all the people answered together and said, 'All that the Lord has spoken we will do!' And Moses brought back the words of the people to the Lord." The marriage was consummated when Moses and the leaders of the tribes of Israel met with God on the top of the mountain, as stated in Exodus 24:1, "Then He said to Moses, 'Come up to the Lord, you and Aaron, Nadab, and Abihu and seventy of the elders of Israel, and you shall worship at a distance.'"

Sadly, the Israelites broke the covenant when they had Aaron make the golden calf. The marriage was reaffirmed through Moses' intercession. Here we see the wedding taking place before God follows through with His promise to Abraham, Isaac, and Jacob to give their descendants the land of Canaan. There is a wedding when God moves forward with His purpose to bring redemption to mankind through His family, the nation of Israel. Just as it happened with Adam and Eve, Israel failed to keep their part of the covenant, but nevertheless God gave many promises of final restoration that He would accomplish through His Son, the Child of Israel and God. Revelation 12 gives a picture of Israel the wife of God bearing His Son in verse 5, "And she gave birth to a son, a male child, who is to rule the nations with a rod of iron; and her child was caught up to God and His throne." This verse is a fulfillment of the prophecy in Psalm 2:7-9 given a thousand years before Revelation was written, "I will surely tell of the decree of the Lord: He said to Me, Thou art My Son, today I have begotten Thee. Ask of Me and I will surely give the nations as Thy inheritance, and the very ends of the earth as Thy possession. Thou shalt break them with a rod of iron, Thou shalt shatter them like earthenware." These verses will be fulfilled in the millennium reign of Christ the Messiah, prophesied in Revelation 20:1-3, "And I saw an angel coming down from heaven, having the key of the abyss and a great chain in his hand. And he laid hold of the dragon, the serpent of old, who is the Devil and Satan, and bound him for a thousand years, and threw him into the abyss, and shut it and sealed it over him, so that he shall not deceive the nations any longer, until the thousand years were completed; after these things he must be released for a short time."

We can be confident that these second coming prophecies will come to pass historically. Why is this true? It is true because we have the historical fulfillment of all the Old Testament prophesies of the coming of Jesus, the Messiah, the first time. If He came the first time as a historical person, verified by biblical eyewitness testimony and secular verification as well, then it stands to reason we can believe He will come the second time in the same way as His first coming.

Cana

The third wedding was at the beginning of Jesus' earthly ministry in the small Galilean town of Cana. It was not far from where He grew up in Nazareth, and was the home of one of His

12 disciples, Nathanael. The wedding was the occasion where Jesus changed the water into wine. This was the first of seven signs of Jesus that John refers to in his gospel. I do not believe it was a matter of happenstance that a miracle at a wedding was used by John to introduce the 3 year ministry of Jesus that would lead to the cross. Nothing in God's Word is a matter of happenstance. It follows the already established precedent that God begins each of His major ongoing works with a wedding.

He began with populating the earth with mankind made in His image for an eternal family of godly seed (Malachi 2:15-16, "God hates divorce"). His family would come through covenant marriage. After Adam and Eve failed their test of obedience in the garden by being deceived to fall into sin by Satan, God began His plan of redemption that He would accomplish through the seed of Abraham, Isaac and Jacob (Israel). To do so He entered into a covenant marriage relationship between Him and the nation of Israel called the Covenant or the Law of Moses at Mount Sinai. Here in John 2:1-11, we see Jesus beginning His 3 year earthly work of redemption by attending a wedding as a guest where He performs His first recorded public miracle.

What is the message of this prophetic picture? The message is one that points to the past and the future. First, the picture points back to the first wedding at the beginning of human history. There we see God officiating in the first wedding after His creative work. In John 2 we see the Son of God as a guest at a wedding to begin His ministry to pay the dowry with His blood for His coming bride, the Church. The miracle of changing the water into wine affirms that Jesus is the same God of the Godhead who created the whole process of changing water (the first formed matter from the elements) into wine (water to soil to vine to grapes to wine). It is good wine, the best wine produced by the good God.

The second point looks to the future wedding when Jesus the Messiah will marry His betrothed bride. The betrothal began at Pentecost when the Church was established by the Holy Spirit through those who first believed the gospel of Jesus' death, burial, and resurrection. As Jesus prepares for His second coming to the earth, the marriage of Jesus and His bride, the Church, takes place in Revelation 19:7, "Let us rejoice and be glad and give glory to Him (God) for the marriage of the Lamb (Jesus) has come and His bride has made herself ready."

Christ and the Church

That brings us to the fourth wedding. As we have already read in Revelation 19:7 before

Jesus returns to earth, there will be a wedding in heaven of Jesus and all true believers who have been raptured prior to the Tribulation described in Revelation. This is a picture of the second Adam (Jesus, 1 Corinthians 15:47) being wed to the second Eve who, like the first Eve, was taken out of the side of Adam. This is in reference to the blood flowing out of Jesus' pierced side on the cross. But, where the first Adam failed, the second Adam (Jesus) was victorious, and through Him, now the Father will have the eternal kingdom He had planned for from the beginning. It will be made up of a family of godly seed produced by obedience and faith out of a free will choice by being born again of the Spirit through faith in Jesus.

The four weddings are a strong example of the consistency of God's Word from beginning to end. What was given as a prophetic picture in the beginning is carried through the scriptures to its fulfillment in the end. Remember we are describing a library of 66 books authored by 40 different men over a period of 4,000 years, in different countries. It is the expression of an eternal, sovereign God guiding its development according to His predetermined plan for His creation. It is a library of books that only God Himself could produce through God-inspired men.

Chapter 4
Miracles

*"Men of Israel, listen to these words,
Jesus the Nazarene, a man attested
to you by God with miracles and
wonders and signs which God
performed through Him in your midst,
just as you yourselves know..."*
Acts 2:22

The theme of this chapter is Miracles. The question I hope to answer in this discourse is why are there miracles in the Bible and how do they contribute to showing the consistency of God's Word with itself from beginning to end? To answer these questions we need to start once again with the beginning of the creation week where we are introduced to God the Creator.

The Why of Miracles

Genesis 1:1 begins the creation account by first introducing us to the God who created things that exist outside of Himself in heaven and earth. The verse starts with, "In the beginning God..." This phrase tells us that God existed before time was created meaning He has always existed eternally. He has no beginning and no end. He exists unlimited by time. He is the Creator of time. The verse then continues with the next phrase, "...God created..." The Hebrew word used here for created is "bara." It is a word that applies to what only God can do; that He called into existence that which did not exist. In other words God created ex nihilo which means "out of nothing." All that exists in the spirit realm or the physical realm was spoken into existence by all powerful God. He willed it all to be so. Finally the verse concludes, "...the heavens and the earth." The heavens would include the highest heaven in the spirit realm and the heavens of earth's atmosphere as well as the space beyond where the sun, moon, planets, and stars dwell. The earth then refers to all the elements made up of atoms that would be formed into all the matter in and on the earth and in the rest of the universe. This verse tells us that God is the great Cause of all that exists outside of Himself. He called it into existence. He is its source of energy as Colossians 1:17 declares,

"He is before all things, and in Him all things hold together." He controls every aspect of every minute function that is necessary for it all to continue to function. This wonderful truth means that He sustains every aspect of what He has created. This Creator God is totally sovereign over all that He has created.

All the above being true makes miracles or supernatural happenings possible, even expected from a sovereign God who is bringing about His purposes for His creation. God uses miracles to distinguish Himself from all other attempts by Satan, fallen angels, or humans to divert attention from Him to themselves as a god. God uses miracles to show He is the one true God.

The major point of all the Old Testament miracles is to prepare the world to believe that Jesus Christ is the Son of the one true God. Not only is He the Son of God, He is God embodied as a man. The Old Testament is all about preparing the way for the coming of Jesus as the Messiah (Christ). Jesus makes this clear in Luke 24:44 that I quoted earlier, "Now He said to them, 'These are my words which I spoke to you while I was still with you, that all things which are written about Me in the Law of Moses and the Prophets and the Psalms must be fulfilled." This verse covers pretty much the different sections found in the Old Testament.

For the rest of this chapter we will look at some miracles in the Old Testament that Jesus mirrors in the New Testament to reveal the fact that He is the same Creator God revealed in the Old Testament thus tying the two together. We will look at miracles in:
- The Law of Moses
- The Prophets
- The Psalms

We will show how Jesus performed similar miracles to Old Testament miracles to prove He is God as He said in John 10:37-38, "If I do not do the works of my Father, do not believe Me; but if I do them, though you do not believe Me (My words), believe the works; that you may know and understand that the Father is in Me, and I in the Father."

The Law of Moses

In the Law of Moses, the first five books of the Bible, we read of the miracle of creation which is the supernatural bringing into existence the natural or physical. Jesus is God in the flesh as John 1:1 states, "In the beginning was the Word (Jesus), and the Word was with God, and the Word was God." Jesus, being a part of the Godhead of creation would have the power to do miracles.

The following are some examples of those similar miracles or creative acts. God spoke the curse of death in Genesis 3. Jesus being God would have authority over death. We read in the gospels that Jesus raised three people from the dead and He arose from the dead Himself. His ability to heal the sick would also express His sovereign power over sickness and disease that are also a result of the death curse. Moses recorded the ten miraculous plagues against Egypt. One such miracle was God changing water into blood. Jesus changed water into wine. God also caused there to be a hail storm. Jesus calmed storms more than once.

There is one other miracle event of many in Jesus' ministry that is tied to Him as being the Creator of Genesis 1 that I want to share. I explained at the beginning of this chapter that God created time, space and matter. In John 6:16-25 John records an event that expresses the power of Jesus as Creator over time, space, and matter. The disciples are in a boat in the middle of the Sea of Galilee in a windstorm. Jesus comes to them walking on the water, gets in the boat, and immediately the boat moves from the middle of the lake to the shore, about three and a half miles. This event records Jesus' authority over the force of gravity by walking on the water. It then shows His power over time, space, and matter when the boat and all that were in it (matter), was moved from the middle of the lake to the shore (space), immediately (time). You can read a description of this miraculous event in Psalm 107:23-30.

The withered fig tree in Mark 11:12-14 and 20-21 refers back to Genesis 2 where God planted the garden with fruit trees. Jesus was staying in Bethany during His final week before the cross and traveled each day to Jerusalem. He became hungry and wanted to eat of a fig tree. The tree had no figs for it was not time for fig season. Jesus cursed the tree anyway. When Jesus was returning to Bethany with His disciples they saw the fig tree was withered from the roots up. There are those who interpret the fig tree to be symbolic of Israel and that may have merit, but I take it back to the Garden of Eden when God planted the garden immediately on the sixth day. The withered tree actually reveals Jesus to be the God who has the power to raise up trees immediately or cause them to wither immediately. But why did Jesus curse the tree if it was not time for figs? It goes back to Genesis 8 after the flood and the beginning of the four seasons. In the original creation before the removal of the water canopy, trees produced year round. Trees producing only in their season is a reminder of God's judgment of the flood and what was lost from God's original perfect creation. We see in scripture the restoration of a year round growing season during the Millennium in Amos 9:13,

"Behold days are coming, declares the Lord, when the plowman will overtake the reaper..." and in the New Heaven and Earth in Revelation 22:2, "...And on either side of the river was the tree of life, bearing twelve kinds of fruit, yielding its fruit every month..." When you look at this miracle in total context of God's word it all fits.

There are other miracles in Moses' book of the law that can be applied to Jesus but the ones listed here suffice to make the point of God's Word being consistent with itself from beginning to end. It begins with the Law of Moses and ends with the grace of God in Christ Jesus who satisfied the Law. It is as John 1:17 states, "For the law was given through Moses; grace and truth were realized through Jesus Christ."

The Prophets

There are many miracles in the Prophets that Jesus mirrors in the gospels. I will use three Old Testament miracles to make this point. The first Old Testament miracle we will look at is found in 2 Kings 4:42-44. A man brought some food to feed one hundred men of Elisha's school of prophets. But there was not nearly enough for all the men to eat. Elisha told his servant to feed them anyway "for the Lord says, 'They shall eat and have some left over.'" So they ate their fill and sure enough there was some left over. This story in the ministry of Elisha foreshadows the miracles of the feeding of five thousand and the feeding of the four thousand by Jesus where in each case there was plenty left over. The two similar miracles show Jesus was far greater than Elisha, and actually is the Lord who made enough food for his 100 prophets. A similar miracle of Elijah and the widow and her son whose flour and oil never ran out can apply here as well.

The second miracle was the healing of Naaman of leprosy. Elisha told him to go and dip in the river Jordan seven times. When he finally did the Bible says, "...his flesh was restored like a child's..." 2 Kings 5:14. Jesus during His ministry healed a leper man by reaching out and touching him. Ten lepers came to Him for healing and he told them to go and present themselves to the priests as commanded in the Law of Moses, Luke 17:11-16. The law of offering for cleansing is found in Leviticus 14. By Jesus requiring them to show themselves to the priests identifies Him as the God who gave that law to Moses.

The third miracle is Jonah and the large fish that swallowed him whole, carried him to shore, and coughed him up so he could run to Nineveh and preach God's warning to them. Jonah was in the belly of the fish for three days without being digested. Jesus refers to this miracle being similar to His being buried in the tomb for three days before His resurrection. But that is not the comparison that I want to make here.

I want to compare Jonah's experience with Matthew 17:24-27 where Jesus tells Peter to go cast a hook in the lake to catch a fish that will have a coin in its mouth that Peter can use to pay a tax. Peter catches the fish and takes the coin to pay the tax just as he was told. How does this miracle compare to Jonah and the large fish? Jonah gets cast into the sea. Then God sent the fish to swallow him and take him on a three day trip to be cast out at the sea shore. In like manner God tells a fish to go to the bottom of the Sea of Galilee, which is one of the deepest lakes in the world, and where many fishing boats had been sunk in storms. The fish was led by God to go to the bottom of the lake and pick up a stater coin worth two drachma (the exact tax amount) out of all the different kinds of coins on the bottom of the lake. The fish was then sent to go and wait to bite on Peter's hook. The two miracles are almost completely the same. They show Jesus to be the sovereign God of both miracles. It is also a reminder of God bringing the animals to the ark showing God's total sovereignty over the animals He created.

There are many miracles in the Old Testament Prophets that parallel the miracles that Jesus performed while here on this earth. John says in John 21:25 that Jesus performed so many miracles and wonders that the whole world could not contain the books that could be written. Thankfully, we have enough books written in God's Word that give us all the information we need to cause us to believe that Jesus is the Christ, the Son of the living God.

The Psalms

The Psalms, because they are hymns and poems not narratives, do not record miracles but at times refer to miracles recorded in accounts in other Old Testament books. In the New Testament Jesus actually quotes verses from the Psalms more than any other Old Testament book. These quotes are used to verify that what was happening in Jesus' life was foreshadowed in the Psalms. These are all considered prophetic miracles made possible by a God that exists outside the limits of time and knows the end from the beginning. The following are some examples of these prophetic miracle Psalms.

In John 6:31-34 the crowd, at a time after Jesus had fed 5,000 people with five loaves and two fish, was asking Jesus for a sign, "Our fathers ate the manna in the wilderness; as it is written, 'He gave them bread out of heaven to eat...'" This is a quote from Psalm 78:24 that refers back to God feeding the Israelites in the wilderness with manna from heaven in Exodus 16. Jesus uses this occasion to make the point that the manna from heaven was a prophetic picture of the real Bread of Life He was going to send from heaven, Jesus Himself. Jesus responds to the crowd by saying, "'Truly, truly, I say to you, it is not Moses who has given you the bread out of heaven. For the bread of God is that which comes down out of heaven, and gives life to the world.' They said therefore to Him, 'Lord evermore give us this bread.' Jesus said to them, 'I am the bread of life; he who comes to Me shall not hunger, and he who believes in Me shall never thirst'" (John 6:32-35).

Toward the end of Jesus' ministry the Jewish leaders were trying to find a way to do away with Jesus. He told them a parable about a vineyard owner who had vine growers who took over the vineyard and refused to pay the owner his due. The Jewish leaders were offended because they knew Jesus was referring to them. When they became angry Jesus quoted to them Psalm 118:21-22 to remind them that their rejection of Him as their Messiah was prophesied by this Psalm when it said, "...The stone which the builders rejected, this became the chief corner stone; this came about from the Lord, and it is marvelous in our eyes." The psalmist was referring here to the Messiah a thousand years before He came and Jesus confirms that fact here.

Jesus, when He was in the Upper Room with His disciples partaking of the Passover meal, prophesied Judas' betrayal that would come later that evening. He quoted Psalm 41:9 to verify that this betrayal was allowed according to God's purpose. The Psalm states, "...He who eats my bread has lifted up his heel against me." Jesus goes on to say, "From now on I am telling you before it comes to pass, so that when it does occur, you may believe that I am He." The "He" Jesus refers to here is the Messiah once again who Psalm 41 speaks of in verses 7-13.

Matthew 21:15-16 records that the chief priest and scribes were angry with Jesus while He was in the temple after His triumphal entry into Jerusalem. They were indignant because He was healing the blind and the lame which caused the children to be yelling out, "Hosanna to the Son of David." The leaders thought this was sacrilegious praising Jesus as God. Jesus responded to them by quoting Psalm 8:2, "...have you never read, 'Out of the mouth of infants and nursing babes Thou hast prepared praise for Thyself?'" This is another confirmation of how the Psalms anticipated Jesus' coming work on earth as the Messiah.

There is one final Psalm Jesus quoted from that is what I call the Crucifixion Psalm. It is Psalm 22. This is a miraculous psalm that seems to have been written by an eyewitness of the crucifixion. Jesus actually quotes from verse 1 while on the cross as a way to remind those observing Him hanging there to remember this psalm. The words He quoted were, "My God, My God, why hast Thou forsaken Me?"

I will not quote the whole psalm but will quote an excerpt that is a very graphic pictorial description of the crucifixion. The verses are 14-18, "I am poured out like water, and all My bones are out of joint; My heart is like wax; it is melted within Me. My Strength is dried up like a potsherd, and My tongue cleaves to My jaws; and thou dost lay Me in the dust of death. For dogs have surrounded Me; a band of evil doers has encompassed Me; they pierced My hands and My feet. I can count all my bones. They look, they stare at Me; they divide My garments among them, and for My clothing they cast lots." The amazing thing about this psalm is that it was written a thousand years before the coming of Jesus, and the Romans did not invent crucifixion until about 500 years after the psalm was written. It is another example of how God said what was going to come and then it came confirming how His Word is consistent with itself, and that God knows the end from the beginning and all the in between. That is why God's Word is miraculous.

Chapter 5
Prophecies

*"...for no prophecy was made by an act
of human will, but men moved by
the Holy Spirit spoke from God."*
2 Peter 1:21

The theme of Prophecies separates the Bible from all other writings in existence. We have already seen how the other themes we have discussed each contain the influence of prophesies. In Isaiah 46:9-10 God Himself declares that having the ability to see the end from the beginning is unique to Him and Him alone; "Remember the former things long past, for I am God, and there is no one like Me, declaring the end from the beginning and from ancient times things which have not been done, saying, 'My purpose will be established, and I will accomplish all My good pleasure; calling a bird of prey from the east, the man of My purpose from a far country. Truly I have spoken; truly I will bring it to pass. I have planned it, surely I will do it.'"

There are many different categories of prophecies. There are short term fulfillments in a matter of a day, some fulfillments in decades, some fulfillments in thousands of years, and some have not been fulfilled yet such as those that refer to the Millennium or New Heaven and New Earth. There are prophecies that apply to one person, a family of people, a nation, many nations, and some to the whole earth. In this chapter we will look at some major Old and New Testament prophecies that tie the two together and make our point that the Bible is consistent with itself from beginning to end; and that the Bible reveals God to be the source of its consistency through His sovereign inspiration. It truly is a miraculous book.

The Flood

The first major prophecy in the Old Testament we will look at is the worldwide flood. God warned Noah of its coming in Genesis 6:13-14, "...The end of all flesh has come before Me, for the earth is filled with violence because of them; and behold I am about to destroy them with the earth. Make for yourself an ark of gopher wood..." Noah began to build the ark and preached of the coming judgment (2 Peter 2:5). The flood came 120 years later. The flood is referred to several times in the

Old Testament such as Psalm 29:10, "The Lord sat as King at the flood..." or Ezekiel 14:14, '...even though these three men, Noah, Daniel, and Job were in its midst, by their own righteousness they could only deliver themselves..."

In the New Testament Jesus spoke of Noah and the flood and compared it to His second coming that is also prophesied by Peter using the flood. Jesus said in Mathew 24:37-39, "For the coming of the Son of Man will be just like the days of Noah. For as in those days which were before the flood they were eating and drinking, they were marrying and giving in marriage, until the day that Noah entered the ark, and they did not understand until the flood came and took them all away, so shall the coming of the Son of Man be." Peter wrote in 2 Peter 3:5-7, "For when they maintain this (mocking the second coming), it escapes their notice that by the Word of God the heavens existed long ago and the earth was formed out of water and by water, through which the world at that time was destroyed, being flooded with water. But the present heavens and earth by His Word are being reserved for fire, kept for the day of judgment and destruction of ungodly men." The second coming then, is fully prophesied by John in Revelation.

The prophecy and event of the flood is a powerful theme that ties the Bible message together from beginning to end. The evidence for a worldwide flood is overwhelming. The strata of the earth's geology has been shown to be laid out by a massive flood. Seventy five percent of all rocks are sedimentary and the others are either volcanic or basement rocks. There are fossils of sea creatures on the tops of mountains, and massive burials of fossilized animals that were all washed together in a heap. Coal beds are massive layers of vegetation that were laid out in layers of floating mats and then buried. All this evidence and much more has been rejected by modern secular scientists, because to accept the worldwide flood would be a validation of the Bible's authenticity; which modern-day atheistic evolution cannot allow.

Abraham and Israel

The next major prophecy we will discuss is God choosing to use Abraham to be the father of His chosen people, Israel. Starting in Genesis 12:1-3 and throughout the rest of the Bible, the Word of God follows God's dealings with Abraham and his descendants through Isaac, and Jacob (Israel) to bring about His redemption of mankind, "Now the Lord said to Abram, 'go forth from your country, and from your relatives and from your father's house, to the land which I will show you; and I will make you a great nation, and I will bless you, and make your name great; and so you shall be a blessing; and I will bless those who bless you, and the one who curses you I will curse. And in you all the families of the earth shall be blessed.'" There are many prophesies to follow in the Bible concerning Abraham and Israel. We will cover only a few.

God told Abraham his descendants would spend 400 years as slaves in Egypt and then God would bring them out by a great deliverance and give them the land of Canaan, Genesis 15:13-14 and 18 says, "And God said to Abram, 'Know for certain that your descendants will be strangers in a land that is not theirs, where they will be enslaved and oppressed four hundred years. But I will also judge the nation whom they will serve; and afterward they will come out with many possessions.'..." to your descendants I will give this land, from the river of Egypt as far as the great river, the river Euphrates...'" This prophecy was given before Isaac and Jacob were born.

Moses records the fulfillment of the above prophecy in the last four books of the Law as well as several others. After Israel enters into covenant with God to be His chosen people, Moses gives them promises of blessings if they obey God and curses if they disobey, predicting they would in time disobey and be sent into captivity. This extensive prophecy is covered from

Deuteronomy 28-30. In Deuteronomy 30:3-4, God gives a promise to bring them out of captivity and restore them as a nation when they repent and turn back to God, "...then the Lord your God will restore you from your captivity, and have compassion on you, and will gather you again from all the peoples where the Lord your God has scattered you. If your outcasts are at the end of the earth, from there the Lord your God will gather you, and from there He will bring you back."

Moving forward in the history of Israel there are three major dispersions that took place. The first came after the apostasy of the northern tribes in 722 B.C. by Sargon II of Assyria; the second was Judah in 605 B.C. by Nebuchadnezzar king of Babylon. The exiles of the northern kingdom never returned. After seventy years of exile, prophesied by Jeremiah in Jeremiah 25:11, the southern kingdom of Judah did return as recorded in the book of Ezra and prophesied by Jeremiah 29:10 once again as before. Daniel 9:13 actually refers back to Deuteronomy 30:3-4 as Daniel prays for Judah after the seventy years were fulfilled, "As it is written in the Law of Moses, all this calamity has come upon us; yet we have not sought the favor of the Lord our God by turning from our iniquity and giving attention to Thy Truth."

Jesus prophesies the third dispersion to come after the destruction of Jerusalem by the Romans in 70 A.D. in Mark 13:2, "...not one stone shall be left upon another which will not be torn down." This is in direct agreement with Daniel 9:26, "Then after the sixty-two weeks the Messiah will be cut off (Crucifixion of Jesus) and have nothing, and the people of the prince who is to come (Tiberius of Rome) will destroy the city and the sanctuary (Herod's temple). And its end will come like a flood; even to the end (second coming of Jesus) there will be war; desolations are determined." After that event of 70 A.D. Judah and the Jews never recovered back to its former self. But the full fulfillment of Deuteronomy 30:3-4 has been taking place since 1948 when Israel was recognized as a nation in their own land. The people of Israel have been returning home ever since that time from all over the world. She is now an economic powerhouse in the world leading in technology development and agricultural markets. God is true to His Word.

Seventy Weeks

The final prophecy I want to discuss is found in Daniel 9:24-27, "Seventy weeks have been decreed for your people (Israel) and your holy city..." This is the prophecy that determines the exact time that the Messiah would come and finish His work of redemption. It is one of the most precise and exact prophecies found in scripture.

The first symbolic sixty-nine week period (7 years equals one week) projects the first coming of the Messiah that would take place 483 years later at Jesus' triumphal entry into Jerusalem. The seventieth week then looks forward to the coming of the Anti-Christ during the tribulation at the end before Christ returns. John MacArthur in his commentary study of the Bible refers to this prophecy as, "...highly complex and startlingly accurate ..." Many other Bible scholars agree. It most definitely is a prophecy like those discussed above that link the Old and New Testaments together in one consistent progress of God's revealed Word and ongoing plan of redemption. All these prophecies are nothing short of miraculous.

Chapter 6
Messiah

*"One of the two who heard John
(the Baptist) speak, and followed Him
(Jesus), was Andrew, Simon Peter's
brother. He found first his own
brother Simon, and said to him,
'We have found the Messiah'..."*
John 1:40-41

The sixth theme we will discuss is that of the Messiah which connects the end of the Bible to the beginning. Messiah means "anointed one," or chosen by God to bring about His redemption of man and God's creation. This chapter is a continuation to the last chapter's theme of prophecies because of the fact that prophecies concerning the Messiah are more prevalent than any other prophetic topic. There are over 300 prophecies concerning the Messiah in the Old Testament.

Seed of the Woman

The Messiah is first predicted as a promise by God to undo the consequences of Adam and Eve's fall into sin because of Satan's deception. The promise is given in Genesis 3:15 when God speaks to Satan and says, "And I will put enmity between you and the woman, and between her seed and your seed; He shall bruise you on the head, and you shall bruise Him on the heel." The "He" is the promised Messiah. The Messiah will be born of the seed of the woman foreshadowing His virgin birth. He will then defeat Satan by crushing his head, while Satan only injures the Messiah but not mortally, foreshadowing the cross and the resurrection.

Seed of Abraham

The next major messianic prophecy is the Messiah coming from the seed of Abraham. God promises Abraham to give the promise land to his seed in Genesis 13:15, "...for all the land which you see, I will give it to you and to your descendants (seed is singular) forever." Also Genesis 17:8 gives the same promise, "And I will give to you and your descendants (seed is singular) after you, the land of your sojourning, all the land of Canaan, for an everlasting possession; and I will be their God." It seems God is referring to all of Abraham's descendants but Paul in Galatians 3:16 tells us the word "seed" in the Hebrew (sometimes translated descendants) refers to the Messiah, "Now the promises were spoken to Abraham and to His seed. He does not say, 'And to seeds,' as referring to many, but rather to one, 'And to your seed', that is Christ (Messiah)." We looked earlier at Abraham's call where God told him, "...and in you all the families of the earth will be blessed." God is referring here to Abraham's seed, the Messiah, who will bring salvation to all of mankind as a blessing.

The seed of Abraham will progress through Isaac and Jacob who then prophesies at the end of his life that the Messiah would come through his son, Judah, in Genesis 49:10, "The scepter shall not depart from Judah, nor the ruler's staff from between his feet, until Shilo comes, and to Him shall be the obedience of the peoples." "Shilo" refers to the Messiah. We can see as the rest of the sentence refers to "Him" who all the people will obey. This prophecy continues as David, a descendant of Judah, is anointed king of Israel. Then he is promised the Messiah will come through his seed. 2 Samuel 7:12 gives this promise, "When your days are complete and you lie down with your fathers, I will raise up your descendent (seed) after you, who will come forth from you, and I will establish His kingdom." This verse is not referring to Solomon. It refers to the Messiah. It is a major verse that caused people in the time of Jesus to refer to Him as the "Son of David." By referring to Him as the Son of David, people were confessing their belief that Jesus is the Messiah.

New Testament Messianic Quotes

In the New Testament there are several verses quoted from the Old Testament showing how Jesus is the fulfillment of all the messianic prophecies. We will cover some of those verses in the rest of this chapter to show how the Messiah theme runs from the beginning to the end of the Bible. The very first chapter of the New Testament, Matthew 1:23, quotes Isaiah 7:14, "Behold the virgin shall be with child, and shall bear a Son, and they shall call His name Immanuel; which translated means, 'God with us'"

Isaiah prophesied the Messiah would come out of Galilee. Jesus grew up in Nazareth and made His home base during His ministry in Capernaum, both of which were in Galilee. This is where the two sons of Jacob, Zebulun and Naphtali received their inheritance. Mathew 4:14-16 quotes Isaiah 9:1, "This was to fulfill what was spoken through Isaiah the prophet saying, 'The land of Zebulun and the land of Naphtali, by the way of the sea, beyond Jordan, Galilee of the Gentiles. The people who were sitting in darkness saw a great light."

Probably the most graphic prophecy in the Old Testament that identifies the Messiah more than any other is Isaiah 53. Each of the gospels allude to this prophecy in one way or another, such as Luke 18:32 that quotes Jesus referring back to Isaiah 53:3, "For He will be delivered up to the Gentiles, and will be mocked and mistreated and spit upon..." Matthew 8:17 quotes Isaiah 53:4, "... He himself took our infirmities, and carried away our diseases." Isaiah 53:7, "...yet He did not open His mouth..." is fulfilled in Mark 14:61, "But he kept silent, and made no answer..." John 1:29, "Behold the Lamb of God who takes away the sins of the world..." alludes to Isaiah 53:6, "All we like sheep have gone astray, each of us has turned to his own way; but the Lord has caused the iniquity of us all to fall on Him."

Matthew 2:6 quotes Micah 5:2 when recording the birth place of Jesus as being prophesied, "and you, Bethlehem, land of Judah; are by no means least among the leaders of Judah; for out of you shall come forth a Ruler, who will shepherd my people Israel." John 12:15 quotes Zechariah 9:9 when recording Jesus' triumphal entry into Jerusalem, "Fear not daughter of Zion; behold your King comes sitting on a donkey's colt."

The Branch

In the Old Testament prophets of Isaiah, Jeremiah and Zechariah, prophecies of the Messiah identify Him as the "Branch." Many verses in the New Testament make a connection between what is said about the Branch and Jesus. Isaiah 11:1 introduces the branch motif, "Then a shoot will spring from the stem of Jesse, and a branch from his root will bear fruit." This branch is obviously referring to the Messiah being the seed coming from Jesse, a descendant of Judah and father of King David. Jeremiah 25:5 gives more information about the Branch, "Behold days are coming, declares the Lord, when I will raise up for David a righteous Branch; and He will reign as King and act wisely and do justice and righteousness in the land." Jeremiah 33:15 restates this same verse.

The prophet Zechariah also refers to the Messiah as the Branch. Isaiah and Jeremiah prophesied before Judah was sent into captivity to Babylon. Zechariah prophesied during the return of Judah back from captivity under the leadership of Zerubbabel and Joshua the high priest to rebuild the temple according to the decree of Cyrus king of the Medes and the Persians. Zechariah 2:8 states, "Now listen, Joshua the high priest, you and your friends who are sitting in front of you--indeed they are men who are a symbol, for behold, I am going to bring in My Servant the Branch." Zechariah 6:12 also speaks of the Branch, "...Thus says the Lord of hosts, 'Behold, a man whose name is Branch, for He will branch out from where He is; and will build the temple of the Lord.'" This temple will be built apparently during the Millennium after the Messiah's second coming.

It seems in the context of each of these Branch prophecies that they are referring to the reign of the Messiah during the Millennium that is prophesied in Revelation 20:3. In the Messiah's first coming He is the suffering Servant, the sacrificial Lamb. In His second coming He is the ruling, reigning King of justice and righteousness as the Branch is portrayed. Revelation 20:6 tells us those who are resurrected in the first resurrection will reign with Christ (Messiah), "Blessed and holy is the one who has a part in the first resurrection; over these the second death has no power, but they will be priests of God and of Christ (Messiah) and will reign with Him (the Branch) for a thousand years."

John 5:39

The Bible is full of prophecies concerning the promised Messiah. That is why Jesus could say to the Jews in John 5:39, "You search the scriptures, because you think that in them you have eternal life; and it is these that bear witness of Me." Also, on the Mount of Transfiguration Moses and Elijah appeared to Jesus while three of His apostles, Peter, James and John were watching. Mark 9:7 then records, "Then a cloud formed, overshadowing them, and a voice came out of the cloud; 'This is My beloved Son, listen to Him.'" This verse confirms what Jesus said in John 5:39 that all the scriptures are about Him. God the Father was telling the three apostles that Jesus is greater than Moses (who symbolizes the Law) and the Prophets (Elijah symbolizes the Prophets) of the Old Testament. He is the fulfillment of all they wrote. They were to listen to Jesus who is the ultimate authority in explaining the true meaning of all of God's Word. That is because the Bible is all about Jesus from beginning to end. No wonder there are more prophecies about the Messiah than any other topic.

The Messiah theme in the Bible is the one theme that ties the whole library of books together more than any other. It is all about Jesus. That is why Revelation 19:13 describes Him as the returning, ruling, reigning King as follows; "And He is clothed with a robe dipped in blood; and His name is called The Word of God." The Messiah is the coming Word of God personified. He is the major theme that makes the Bible consistent with itself. That is miraculous!

Chapter 7
Redemption

*"But when these things begin to take place,
straighten up and lift up your heads,
because your redemption is drawing near."*
Luke 21:28

Redemption is the final major theme of the Bible we will discuss. What does redemption mean? It is the process of buying back or winning back something that had been lost or taken away. In the case of the Bible, redemption is the process God is developing in history through the Seed of the woman to Abraham's Seed, the Seed of David, the Messiah. The Messiah would shed His blood to buy back the creation lost to Satan's deception of the man, Adam; who was given dominion of that creation. The redemption process began with God's curse on Satan in Genesis 3:15 where He promised the Seed of the woman would crush the head of the seed of the serpent (Satan the devil).

The Exodus

The prophetic picture of God's redemption of mankind is given through the account of the Exodus of His chosen people, Israel, out of slavery in Egypt. Redemption is also shown in Israel's return to the land of Canaan that God promised to give to the descendants of Abraham, Isaac, and Jacob over four hundred years before. The prophetic message of the Exodus is that man is lost in slavery to sin and God sent Jesus to buy us back out of sin with His blood. He did this so He can take us to the promise land in heaven; for the Law stated in Leviticus 17:11 that, "life is in the blood" and only blood can atone for sin. Paul, in Hebrews 9:22 stated it this way, "... and without shedding of blood there is no forgiveness." Jesus paid the price of our redemption out of sin with His blood; that is why He is called the Redeemer in the prophecy of the Messiah in Isaiah 59:20, "And a Redeemer will come to Zion, and to those who turn from transgression (who repent) in Jacob, declares the Lord."

Ruth

The Law contains prophetic pictures of redemption in Leviticus 25 and 27. The book of Ruth is a story of redemption in the life of the history of King David's family. Boaz, the great grandfather of David, was the redeemer of Ruth, the widow of Naomi's son, whose father was a kinsman of Boaz. Boaz could redeem and restore Ruth's husband's inheritance because he was a blood relative of her husband. The application of the story is Jesus, as our blood relative (a man born of a woman), is our Kinsman Redeemer who has restored our inheritance as children of God through His sinless blood.

Jesus the Redeemer

Many books in the Old Testament contain the concept of redemption and the Messiah Redeemer, such as Psalm 78:35, "And they remembered that God was their rock, and the Most High God their Redeemer." The same is true in the New Testament. There are several passages that refer to Jesus as our Redeemer. Zacharias, the priestly father of John the Baptist, proclaims God's promise of redemption was to come through His Messiah. Zacharias' son, John, was born to introduce the Messiah to the world. Zacharias prophesied after John the Baptist was born in Luke 1:68-70, "Blessed be the God of Israel, for He has visited us and accomplished redemption for His people, and has raised up a horn of salvation for us in the house of David His servant--as He spoke by the mouth of His Holy prophets from of old…"

Paul and Peter

Paul, in Galations 3:13-14 refers to redemption, "Christ (Messiah) redeemed us from the curse of the Law (The person who sins will die Ezekiel 18:20), having become a curse for us--for it is written, 'Cursed is everyone who hangs on a tree-- in order that in Christ Jesus the blessing of Abraham (Genesis 12:3) might come to the Gentiles..." The Gentiles refers to all other peoples beyond those of Israel. Peter in 1 Peter 1:18 refers to redemption, "...knowing that you were not redeemed with perishable things like silver or gold from your futile way of life inherited from your forefathers, but with precious blood, as of a lamb unblemished and spotless, the blood of Christ." The unblemished Lamb Peter writes of refers back to the Passover lamb requirement in Exodus 12:5, "Your lamb must be an unblemished male a year old..." The Passover lamb is another prophetic picture of the coming Messiah to bring God's redemption to mankind from slavery to sin just as He redeemed Israel from slavery in Egypt.

Revelation

The theme of redemption culminates in Revelation 5:9 where the Lamb talked about in verse 6 is being praised with a song of praise for His victory over death that won Him the right to break the seven seals of God's final judgment scroll. The praise song sings, "Worthy art Thou to take the book (scroll), and to break its seals; for Thou wast slain, and did purchase (redeem) for God with Thy blood men from every tribe and tongue and people and nation." Jesus is the Lamb they are singing about who is the Messiah that accomplished the redemption of mankind and God's creation. As in the other themes of the Bible we have discussed, the redemption theme ties all of God's Word together in one ongoing story from beginning to end. God's Word is miraculous!

The redemption of the world has already taken place. It was accomplished by Jesus Christ when He shed His blood and died on the cross 2,000 years ago. The redemption price has been paid for every person who has or will ever live. But each of us as free moral agents cannot be forced to receive that redemption as a free gift. We each have to choose to receive it. To do so, we must do four things.

First, we must know that we have sinned against God. Second, we must be grieved in our hearts because we know we have offended God. Third, we must confess our sinfulness to God and ask Him for His forgiveness. Fourth, we must believe that Jesus Christ is the Son of God, who paid the price for our redemption; and then invite Him into our hearts to take control of our lives. If you have done these four things, then you have been redeemed by the blood of the Lamb. Here is God's promise found in Romans 10:13, "... for WHOEVER WILL CALL ON THE NAME OF THE LORD WILL BE SAVED." The "Lord" is Jesus and "saved" is redeemed. I pray you have chosen to do these four things.

Conclusion

The Bible is a miraculous library of books because it is the Word of God. He is not just any god but the one true God who is eternal without beginning or end. He is the One who exists outside of time and He is the Creator of time. He is all powerful, all knowing, all wise, all righteous, merciful and good. He is the only Being that has the ability to oversee the inspiration of a book (the Bible) of 66 different books. These books were written over a period of 4,000 years, by forty different men living in different times, places, and cultures. Yet it contains common major themes from the beginning to the end. The Bible reads as one ongoing historical revelation that is totally consistent with itself. Only the God revealed in the Bible could bring it into existence.

All the above seven themes and many others give us confidence that the Bible is the true Word of God. But its greatest witness and authority is the historical Jesus of Nazareth. Why? Because He claimed to be God Himself who came to His creation to live in it as a man. If that is true, and I believe it is from much evidence, then Jesus is the historical eyewitness to all that is recorded in the Bible and He is its ultimate authority of authenticity. It was written about Him, and by Him; just as He said to the Jews in John 5:39, "You search the Scriptures, because you think that in them you have eternal life; and it is these that bear witness of Me..." How can we trust all this is true? We can do so because of the historical eye witness account of His resurrection from the dead. The historical resurrection of Jesus Christ validates all the rest of the Bible. It is well documented by several sources besides the four Gospels and over 500 witnesses. Jesus told the Jewish leaders in John 2:19: "Destroy this temple (His physical body) and in three days I will raise it up." They did and He did. They killed Him on the cross and three days later He arose from the dead just like He said He would. Only God could do that. So all that is recorded in the Bible is confirmed by Jesus and He is our ultimate authority. Why? Jesus was present during every aspect of what the Bible has recorded by men who were inspired by His Spirit from beginning to end.

The Bible should be read with faith to believe it is true. It should be read over and over again to gain new insights. The Bible can be trusted to fulfill all of its promises. Why? The Bible is inspired by the one true God who is the Truth and He cannot lie. Because this is true Paul could tell his disciple, Timothy, with all confidence, "All Scripture is inspired by God and is profitable for teaching, for reproof, for correction, for training in righteousness..." 2 Timothy 3:15. So just believe God's Word. Live by it as your guide and it will take you to an eternal realization of all that you were created to be and enjoy with your Creator, Redeemer, and Lord, the God of the miraculous Bible.

It is as Jeremiah 29:11 promised, " For I know the plans that I have for you, declares the Lord, plans for welfare and not calamity to give you a future and a hope..." And, it is what Paul quoted in 1 Corinthians 2:9 from Isaiah 64:4, "Things which eye has not seen and ear has not heard, and which have not entered the heart of man, all that God has prepared for those who love Him."

Here is God's promise to all those who read and believe His Word:

"So shall My word be which goes forth from My mouth; it shall not return to Me empty, without accomplishing what I desire, and without succeeding in the matter for which I sent it," Isaiah 55:11.! **GOD SAID IT, HE IS DOING IT, SO BE IT!**

God's Word is Miraculous!

God's Word

The Word of God
Beats all the odds
From beginning to end
Over thousands of years
It beats the attacks
On all of its facts
From creation
To consummation
Beginning to end.
It withstands every test
By men to outguess
What it records to be true;
Yet believed by so few.
But those who believe
Know what will be;
That God will retrieve
All Adam had lost
But at a terrible cost.
It's all written there
The truth that's laid bare
For all who will read
While God plants His seed
In the soil of hearts
Ready to receive, God's Word

By Steve Kern 5/11/2020

Appendix

The following is a list of 10 other books written by Dr. Steve Kern:

The Eden's Veil Trilogy:

Eden's Veil:

A fictional story that takes place before the flood about a man searching for truth in a hostile world controlled by the false god, Lucifer. Baqash goes on a quest to search for the Garden of Eden and the Line of Light in the pre-flood environment of dinosaurs and giants.

Eden's Son:

The hero, Baqash goes on an adventure to return to his home to tell his father and the city he rules about the one true God. He has become a fugitive enemy of the Lucifer cult.

Eden's Tears:

The Baqash life story picks up where he has become an older man and the son of his friend Lamech, whose name is Noah, prepares an ark for the coming flood. It follows Noah's family building the ark, surviving the flood in the ark and their new life after coming off of the ark.
The trilogy is written for 8th grade and above and contains many life lessons.

Judgment's Greatest Question:

This book is a series of messages inspired by Isaiah 58 that describes God's chosen fast. It is a challenge for Christians to live their lives as servants following the example of Jesus.

No Other Gods:

A commentary on the first eleven chapters of Genesis from a young earth, literal historical perspective. It gives many of the arguments from science, apologetics, archeology, and ancient sources that support the young earth interpretation of the Bible.

The Existence of God:

Gives a summary explanation of the apologetic arguments for the existence of God with reliable sources.

God's Answer to the Question of Evil:

Explains from Genesis how evil can exist in a fallen world created by a good God.

God's Purposes for Marriage:

This book was written in response to the U.S. Supreme Court's decision to legalize same-sex marriage. It gives God's original intent for establishing marriage from the biblical account given in Genesis.

Genuine Christianity:

A study from 1 John 4 to show what true Christians are supposed to look like by the way they live as followers of Jesus.

From My Heart to Your Hand:

A booklet of poems on various subjects.